CW01281402

Keto Starter Guide

Enjoy Over 50 Super Easy And Tasty Recipes
To Start Your Transformation

Elena Fields

© **Copyright 2021 - All rights reserved.**

The content contained within this book may not be reproduced, duplicated or transmitted without direct written permission from the author or the publisher.

Under no circumstances will any blame or legal responsibility be held against the publisher, or author, for any damages, reparation, or monetary loss due to the information contained within this book. Either directly or indirectly.

Legal Notice:

This book is copyright protected. This book is only for personal use. You cannot amend, distribute, sell, use, quote or paraphrase any part, or the content within this book, without the consent of the author or publisher.

Disclaimer Notice:

Please note the information contained within this document is for educational and entertainment purposes only. All effort has been executed to present accurate, up to date, and reliable, complete information. No warranties of any kind are declared or implied. Readers acknowledge that the author is not engaging in the rendering of legal, financial, medical or professional advice. The content within this book has been derived from various sources. Please consult a licensed professional before attempting any techniques outlined in this book.

By reading this document, the reader agrees that under no circumstances is the author responsible for any losses, direct or indirect, which are incurred as a result of the use of information contained within this document, including, but not limited to, errors, omissions, or inaccuracies.

Table Of Contents

DESCRIPTION 8
INTRODUCTION 10
BREAKFAST 12
1. EASY LOW CARB KETO BREAKFAST CASSEROLE 12
2. LOW-CARB STUFFED POBLANO PEPPERS 14
3. SPAGHETTI SQUASH WITH CRISPY SAGE GARLIC SAUCE 15
4. LOW CARB ORANGE DREAMLIKE SMOOTHIE 17
5. HOLLEY'S HAM AND SWISS BREAKFAST MUFFINS 18
MAINS 20
6. MUSHROOM RISOTTO 20
7. ASPARAGUS RISOTTO 22
8. BALSAMIC VEGETABLE KABOBS 24
SIDES 26
9. GARLIC MARINATED MUSHROOMS 26
10. GREEN BEANS AND TUNA SALAD 27
11. GROUND TURKEY COCKTAIL BITES 29
12. PANEER CHEESE WRAPPED WITH PROSCIUTTO 31
SEAFOOD 34
13. SOUR AND SWEET FISH WITH CIDER AND STEVIA 34
14. FANCY SALMON AND EGG SALAD 36
15. OMEGA3 SALMON AND JALAPENO SALAD 38
16. ROASTED VEGETABLES WITH SALMON 40
POULTRY 42
17. LEMONY WHOLE ROASTED TURKEY 42
18. DELICIOUS CHICKEN FAJITA MEAL WITH TORTILLA 44
19. DELICIOUS CHICKEN THIGHS WITH TOMATO AND RED PEPPER 46

MEAT		48
20.	EASY PAN-FRIED SKIRT STEAK	48
21.	CHEESEBURGER SOUP WITH HERBS	50
22.	BACON-WRAPPED MEATBALLS	52
KETO PIZZA AND PASTA		54
23.	PESTO PARMESAN TEMPEH WITH GREEN PASTA	54
24.	CREAMY TOFU WITH GREEN BEANS AND KETO FETTUCCINE	56
25.	DELICIOUS SAMBAL SEITAN NOODLES	59
VEGANS & VEGETARIANS		62
26.	STIR FRY TURNIP GREENS	62
27.	LEMON DILL GRILL TURNIPS	64
28.	STIR FRIED CABBAGE	65
29.	CREAMY AVOCADO ZOODLES	66
EGGS & DIARY		68
30.	CHEESE CHIPS ASIAGO	68
31.	CAULIFLOWER MAC AND CHEESE	70
VEGETABLES		72
32.	VEGAN KETO PORRIDGE	72
33.	CINNAMON FAUX-ST CRUNCH CEREAL	74
34.	KETO MUFFINS	76
35.	CAPRESE GRILLED EGGPLANT ROLL- UPS	77
SOUP, STEWS, BROTHS & SAUCES		80
36.	EGGS TOMATO SAUCE	80
37.	COCONUT ASPARAGUS SOUP	82
38.	PARMESAN FENNEL SOUP	84
39.	LUSCIOUS CHICKEN THIGH STEW	85
40.	FISH GINGER SOUP	87

SALADS		88
41.	CLASSIC TZATZIKI CHICKEN SALAD	88
SAUCES, DRESSING & DIP		90
42.	FRESH MUSHROOM SAUCE	90
SNACKS		92
43.	SPICY MUFFINS	92
44.	KETO GIN COCKTAIL	94
45.	PARMESAN AND GARLIC KETO CRACKERS	95
DESSERTS		98
46.	LIME RHUBARB AND PLUMS MOUSSE	98
47.	AVOCADO AND GRAPES MOUSSE	99
48.	NUTMEG DATES MOUSSE	100
49.	COCONUT, WATERMELON AND AVOCADO MOUSSE	101
50.	BUTTERSCOTCH PUDDING POPSICLES	102
31-DAY MEAL PLAN		104
CONCLUSION		108

DESCRIPTION

Keto diet is a low carb high fat and a moderate amount of protein diet. Normally our body uses glucose as a primary source of energy. This glucose is stored in our body muscles and tissues into the form of glycogens. When glycogen levels are increased then excess glycogens are converted and stored into the form of fats.

Keto diet is a low carb diet when you restrict carb it will decrease the glycogen level and also decrease hormonal insulin level into our body. Due to low carb intake, your body burns fats for energy. During this process, fatty acids are released from stored fats and converted into ketones. It is one kind of acid travel through your bloodstream. Your body muscles and tissues use it as a fuel. Ketone The Ketogenic diet is a diet that focuses on reducing your carbohydrate intake and makes you eat more healthy fats. It is also a diet that has been proven not only to help lose pounds but also

I am so excited that you have chosen to take a new path using the Ketogenic diet plan. The plan is recognized by several names, including the low-carb diet, Ketogenic low-carbohydrate diet & high-fat (LCHF diet plan, and the Keto diet.

Your liver produces ketones, which are used as energy to provide sufficient levels of protein. The process of ketosis is natural and occurs daily – no matter the total of carbs consumed. provide near about 70 percent of your daily brain energy needs.

This book covers the following topics:

- Breakfast
- Mains
- Sides
- Seafood
- Poultry
- Meat
- Vegetables
- Soups and stews
- Snacks
- Desserts and more!!!

INTRODUCTION

Keto diet is not just a diet it is healthy eating habit comes with various health benefits.

- Rapid weight loss

This is one of the major benefits of the keto diet. Keto diet is basically a low carb diet, due to this your body glucose level is decreased and your body breaks down fats for energy. This will reduce your weight rapidly. Keto diet provides long term weight loss benefits.

- Help to maintain your blood sugar level

When you are on a keto diet your body uses ketones for energy instead of glucose. These ketones don't need insulin to transport into your body cell. It indicates that a keto diet is insulin resistance and helps to maintain your blood sugar level.

- Improves your brain functions

Keto diet helps to improve your brain health and brain functions. When you are on a keto diet your body uses ketones for energy. These ketones fill full 70 percent of brain energy needs. Most of the scientific research and study proves that a keto diet helps to reduce the risk of brain-related conditions like Alzheimer's,

Parkinson's, epilepsy etc.

- Anti-aging properties

Keto diet is insulin resistance, it reduces the insulin level into your body. It helps to reduce oxidative stress and helps to increase your lifespan. Due to low calorie it helps to slow down your aging process.

- Improves your athletic performance

Keto diet helps to reduce your body weight rapidly. Most of the scientific research shows that a keto diet reduces your body fat and helps to maintain your muscle mass. It improves your athletic performance.

BREAKFAST

1. Easy Low Carb keto Breakfast Casserole

Preparation Time: 10minutes

Cooking Time: 45 Minutes Serving: 12

INGREDIENTS

- 1 pound breakfast sausage
- 1 tsp Garlic and 12 Eggs
- 1/2 cup Yellow onion
- 3 cups Spinach
- 1/8tsp salt, pepper, 2 cups peppers
  - 1/2 cup Cheddar cheese

DIRECTIONS

1. Preheat stove to 350 degrees F and set up a heating dish with non-stick cooking shower and put in a safe spot.
2. Ground and cook wiener in a skillet until completely cooked. Include garlic, peppers, and onions to the skillet and sauté with frankfurter for 2 minutes. Spot this in your readied heating dish.
3. In a different bowl whisk eggs with salt and pepper,

pour egg wash over vegetables in a heating dish and tenderly blend to ensure eggs are covering the whole dish.

4. Top with cheddar and heat for 45 minutes or until a fork can confess all and eggs are cooked completely through.

NUTRITION: Calories 210, Fat 16g, Carbs 3g, Sugar 2g, Protein 13g

2. Low-Carb Stuffed Poblano Peppers

Preparation Time: 15minutes

Cooking Time: 30 Minutes Serving: 1

INGREDIENTS

- 1 poblano pepper
- 1/3 cup finely chopped cauliflower
- 1/3 lb ground beef
- 1 tsp onion
- 3 tsp tomato sauce

DIRECTIONS

1. Cut the poblano pepper down the middle and take out the seeds.
2. Dark colored the ground hamburger and onion in a little skillet.
3. Blend the ground hamburger blend with the cauliflower and tomato sauce.
4. Spoon into the pepper parts

NUTRITION: Calories 344, Fat 25g, Carbs 12g, Sugar 4g, Protein 28g

3. Spaghetti Squash with Crispy Sage Garlic Sauce

Preparation Time: 5minutes

Cooking Time: 15 Minutes Serving: 4

INGREDIENTS

- 1 medium spaghetti squash
- 1 cup water and 1 small bunch fresh sage
- 3-5 cloves garlic
- 2 tsp olive oil
- 1 tsp salt
- ⅛ teaspoon nutmeg

DIRECTIONS

1. Divide the squash and scoop out the seeds.
2. Include water into the weight cooker and lower the squash parts looking up - stacking them one over the other, if necessary.
3. Close and lock the top of the weight cooker. Cook for 3-4 minutes at high weight.
4. Meanwhile, in a virus saute dish includes savvy, garlic, and olive oil. Cook the oil blend on low warmth, mixing incidentally to cook the savvy leaves. At the point when time is up, open the cooker by discharging the weight.

5. Coax the squash strands out of the shell utilizing a fork and thud them into the sauté' skillet.
6. When the entirety of the squash is there turn off the warmth, sprinkle with salt

and nutmeg, at that point swoosh everything around to blend well.

NUTRITION: Calories: 88.6, Fat 4g, Carbs 13.8g, Sugar 5g, Protein 1.5g

4. Low Carb Orange Dreamlike Smoothie

Preparation Time: 5 Minutes Serving: 1

INGREDIENTS

- 16 ounces unsweetened almond milk
- 1 packet artificial sweetener
- 4 ounces heavy cream
- 1 scoop Jay Robb Tropical Dreamlike Whey powder
- 1/2 cup crushed ice

INSTRUCTIONS

1. Put all Ingredients in blender and mix until smooth. This formula duplicates well.

NUTRITION: Calories 290, Fat 25g, Carbs 4g, Sugar 2g, Protein 15g

5. Holley's Ham and Swiss Breakfast Muffins

Preparation Time: 10 minutes

Cooking Time: 25 Minutes Serving: 4

INGREDIENTS

- Eggs
- 1/2 cup grated Swiss cheese
- oz. Canadian Bacon
- 1/4 Cup Salsa, Salt, and Pepper
- 3 Baby Bella Mushrooms

DIRECTIONS

1. Preheat broiler to 350° and shower a biscuit skillet with a non-stick cooking splash or gently oil.
2. In an enormous blending bowl, pound up the 3 cheddar wedges with a fork. Split every one of the 6 eggs into the bowl and blend well in with the cheddar.
3. Include Canadian bacon, mushrooms, salsa, and a touch of salt and pepper to the bowl and combine all Ingredients.
4. Spoon blend into biscuit dish – This clump will fill 8 of the 12 spots in the biscuit skillet.

5. Heat for 25 minutes. Serve and Enjoy

NUTRITION: Calories: 250, Fat 26g, Carbs 4g, Sugar 3g, Protein 7g

MAINS

6. Mushroom Risotto

Preparation Time: 15 minutes

Cooking Time: 15 minutes Serving: 2

INGREDIENTS

- 2 cups cauliflower
- 1 tablespoon olive oil
- ¼ cup mushrooms, sliced
- 1/2 cup vegetable broth
- 2 tablespoon heavy cream
- Salt and black pepper to taste

DIRECTIONS

1. Start by grinding the cauliflower florets in a food processor to make rice.
2. Now sauté mushrooms with oil in a skillet until soft.
3. Toss in cauliflower rice, and mix well.
4. Pour in the stock, and cook for 10 minutes approximately until soft.

5. Stir in cream, salt, and black pepper.
6. Serve fresh and warm.

NUTRITION: Calories 324 Total Fat 13.6 g Saturated Fat 5.1 g Cholesterol 129 mg Sodium 55 mg Total Carbs 6.2 g Fiber 2.4 g Sugar 0.7 g Protein 3.4 g

7. Asparagus Risotto

Preparation Time: 15 minutes

Cooking Time: 15 minutes Serving: 2

INGREDIENTS

- 2 cups cauliflower
- 1 tablespoon olive oil
- ¼ asparagus, cut into ½ inch pieces
- 1/2 cup vegetable broth
- 2 tablespoons. heavy cream
- Salt and black pepper to taste

DIRECTIONS

1. Start by grinding the cauliflower florets in a food processor to make rice.
2. Now sauté asparagus with oil in a skillet for 3 minutes.
3. Toss in cauliflower rice, and mix well.
4. Pour in the stock, and cook for 10 minutes approximately until soft.
5. Stir in cream, salt, and black pepper.

6. Serve fresh and warm.

NUTRITION: Calories 311 Total Fat 0.5 g Saturated Fat 2.4 g Cholesterol 69 mg Sodium 58 mg Total Carbs 1.4 g Fiber 0.7 g Sugar 0.3 g
Protein 1.4 g

8. Balsamic Vegetable Kabobs

Preparation Time: 15 minutes
Cooking Time: 10 minutes Serving: 3

INGREDIENTS

- 1 tablespoon olive oil or butter
- 1/2 cup red bell pepper, diced into squares
- ½ cup zucchini, thickly sliced
- ½ cup yellow onion, cut into squares
- 1 tablespoon balsamic vinegar
- Salt and black pepper to taste

DIRECTIONS

1. Start by toss all the vegetables, olive oil, salt, black pepper and vinegar in a bowl.
2. Now thread the balsamic vegetables on the skewers alternately.
3. Prepare and preheat the grill on medium heat.
4. Grill the vegetable skewers for 2-4 minutes per side until al dente.
5. Serve fresh and warm.

NUTRITION: Calories 319 Total Fat 20 g Saturated Fat 7.3 g Cholesterol 102 mg Sodium 192 mg Total Carbs 3.1 g Sugar 1 g Fiber 2.1 g Protein 13.1 g

SIDES

9. Garlic Marinated Mushrooms

Servings: 8

Preparation: 5 minutes

Cooking: 60 minutes

INGREDIENTS

- 2 1/2 cups fresh white mushrooms
- 2 cups vinegar (distilled
- 6 cloves garlic
- 1/2 tsp salt

DIRECTIONS

1. Soak mushrooms in distilled vinegar, chopped garlic and salt for about one hour.
2. Remove mushrooms from the pot and place in colander to drain.
3. Keep refrigerated.

NUTRITION: Calories: 21 Carbohydrates: 2g Proteins: .8g Fat: 0.1g Fiber: .3g

10. Green Beans and Tuna Salad

Servings: 8

Preparation: 10 minutes

Cooking Time: 20 minutes

INGREDIENTS

- 3/4 cup of green beans, boiled
- 1 cucumber
- 1 small green hot pepper
- 1 avocado
- 1 large zucchini
- Juice and zest of 2 limes
- 3 Tbsp of olive oil
- Salt and ground black pepper
- 2 can (11 oz tuna fish
- 3 Tbsp of sesame seeds
- 2 Tbsp of fresh mint, finely chopped

DIRECTIONS

1. Place green beans in a large salad bowl.
2. Cut the cucumber in half, and then in slices.
3. Clean and slice the pepper, avocado, zucchini and put in a salad bowl; gently stir to combine.

4. Season the salad with the salt and pepper, and pour the lime juice, lime zest and olive oil; toss to combine.
5. Finally, add tuna fish over salad.
6. Sprinkle with sesame and fresh mint and refrigerate for 20 minutes.
7. Serve.

NUTRITION: Calories: 414 Carbohydrates: 6.5g Proteins: 57g Fat: 17.5g Fiber: 3g

11. Ground Turkey Cocktail Bites

Servings: 6

Preparation: 10 minutes

Cooking: 5 minutes

INGREDIENTS

- 2 cups ground turkey breast
- 3 Tbsp mayonnaise
- 2 Tbsp grated onion
- 1/2 tsp celery salt
- 2 Tbsp fresh parsley finely chopped
- 1 tsp of garlic powder
- 1/2 tsp of Tabasco sauce
- 3 Tbsp ground almonds
- Lemon wedges For serving

DIRECTIONS

1. In a large bowl, combine all Ingredients in compact mixture.
2. Refrigerate for 2 hours.
3. Shape the turkey mixture into small bite- size pieces.
4. Heat one nonstick frying pan and cook turkey balls for 5 minutes or until crisp.

5. Serve hot with lemon wedges.

NUTRITION: Calories: 209 Carbohydrates: 3g Proteins: 38.2 Fat: 5.3g Fiber: .5g

12. Paneer Cheese Wrapped with Prosciutto

Servings: 6

Preparation: 5 minutes

Cooking: 5 minutes

INGREDIENTS

- 1/2 lbs. of Paneer cheese (or use tofu as a substitute
- 6 thin slices of prosciutto
- 1 Tbsp of fresh chopped oregano
- 3 Tbsp of extra-virgin olive oil
- Lemon wedges For serving

DIRECTIONS

1. Cut cheese in 6 sticks.
2. Sprinkle chopped oregano over cheese sticks.
3. Wrap each cheese stick with a strip of prosciutto, and then drizzle with olive oil.
4. Heat one nonstick skillet and fry cheese sticks with prosciutto for about one minute on each side.

5. Serve hot with lemon wedges.

NUTRITION: Calories: 242 Carbohydrates: 4g Proteins: 25g Fat: 14.5g Fiber: .3g

SEAFOOD

13. Sour and Sweet Fish with Cider and Stevia

Preparation time: 5 minutes

Cooking Time: 15 minutes Servings: 2

INGREDIENTS

- ¼ cup unsalted butter, melted
- 1lb fish chunks
- Salt and freshly cracked black pepper, to taste
- 2 drops of stevia
- 1 tbsp apple cider vinegar

INSTRUCTIONS:

1. Take a skillet pan, place it over medium heat, add butter and when it melts, add fish and cook for 3 minutes.
2. Then season fish with salt and black pepper, add stevia and vinegar, stir until mixed and cook for 10 minutes.
3. Serve straight away.

4. For meal prep, let fish cool completely, then distribute evenly between two air-tight containers and store in the refrigerator for up to two days.
5. When ready to eat, reheat fish in the microwave until hot and then serve.

NUTRITION: Calories 258, Total Fat 16.7g, Total Carbs 2.8g, Protein 24.5g, Sugar 2.7g, Sodium 649mg

14. Fancy Salmon and Egg Salad

Preparation time: 3 hours and 5 minutes

Cooking Time: 0 minutes

Servings: 2

INGREDIENTS

- 6oz cooked salmon, chopped
- ½ of medium white onion, peeled, chopped
- 2 stalks of celery, chopped
- 4 organic eggs, hard-boiled, peeled, cubed
- 1 tbsp fresh dill, chopped
- Salt and freshly cracked black pepper, to taste
- ¾ cup avocado mayonnaise

INSTRUCTIONS:

1. Take a large bowl, add salmon in it, then add remaining Ingredients and stir until well combined.
2. Cover the bowl with a plastic wrap and then refrigerate for a minimum of 3 hours before serving.
3. For meal prep, transfer salmon salad into an airtight container and store in the refrigerator for up to 3 days.

4. When ready to eat, reheat salmon in the microwave until hot and then serve.

NUTRITION: Calories 303, Total Fat 30g, Total Carbs 1.7g, Protein 10.3g, Sugar 1g, Sodium 314mg

15. Omega3 Salmon and Jalapeno Salad

Preparation time: 5 minutes

Cooking Time: 10 minutes

Servings: 2

INGREDIENTS

- ½lb salmon fillet, skinless, cut into 4 steaks
- ¼ tbsp lime juice
- 1 tbsp olive oil, divided
- 4 tbsp sour cream
- ¼ of zucchini, cut into small cubes
- ¼ tsp jalapeño pepper, seeded, chopped
- Salt and freshly cracked black pepper, to taste
- ¼ tbsp fresh dill, chopped

INSTRUCTIONS:

1. Take a skillet pan, place it over medium heat, add oil and when hot, add salmon and cook for 5 minutes per side.
2. Then season salmon with salt and black pepper, stir well, and then transfer to a plate.

3. Place remaining Ingredients in a bowl, stir well, then top it over salmon and serve.

NUTRITION: Calories 291, Total Fat 21.1g, Total Carbs 2.5g, Protein 23.1g, Sugar 0.6g, Sodium 112mg

16. Roasted Vegetables with Salmon

Preparation time: 15 minutes

Cooking Time: 16 minutes Servings: 3

INGREDIENTS

- 1 cup of water
- 2 cups broccoli florets
- 3 fillets of salmon
- 1 tbsp lemon juice
- 1/4 tsp garlic powder
- Salt and freshly cracked black pepper to taste
- ½ tsp cumin powder
- 1/4 tsp red chili powder
- 1 tbsp olive oil

INSTRUCTIONS:

1. Switch on the instant pot, pour in water, insert a trivet stand, place broccoli on it, and shut with the lid.
2. Press the 'steam' button, cook it for 10 minutes at high-pressure setting, and when instant pot beeps, do quick pressure release.
3. Then open the instant pot, transfer broccoli to a dish and let cool for 10 minutes.
4. Meanwhile, place salmon fillets in a shallow dish, drizzle

with lemon juice, and then sprinkle with garlic, salt, black pepper, cumin, and red chili powder.

5. Drain the instant pot, press the 'sauté' button, grease the inner pot with oil, then add salmon in it and cook for 3 minutes per side until seared.
6. For meal prep, distribute vegetables and salmon between three air-tight containers, and the store in the refrigerator for up to three days.
7. When ready to eat, reheat vegetables and salmon in the microwave until hot and then serve.

NUTRITION: Calories 348, Total Fat 17.5g, Total Carbs 21.2g, Protein 26.5g, Sugar 4.6g, Fiber 10.3g, Sodium 561mg,

POULTRY

17. Lemony Whole Roasted Turkey

Preparation time: 10 minutes

Cooking Time: 4 hours and 30 minutes

Servings: 6

INGREDIENTS

- 2lb whole Turkey, cleaned, pat dried
- 2 tbsp lemon juice
- Salt and freshly cracked black pepper, to taste
- 4 cloves of garlic, peeled
- ¼ cup shredded cheddar cheese

INSTRUCTIONS:

1. Prepare the turkey and for this, stuff the turkey cavity with garlic and then season with salt and black pepper.
2. Switch on the crockpot, place turkey in it, drizzle with lemon juice and cook for 3 to hours at high heat setting until thoroughly cooked.

3. Then sprinkle cheese on turkey, continue cooking for 30 minutes until cheese has melted and serve.

NUTRITION: Calories 310, Total Fat 12.8g, Total Carbs 0.5g, Protein 45.3g, Sugar 0.1g, Sodium 230mg

18. Delicious Chicken Fajita Meal with Tortilla

Preparation time: 10 minutes

Cooking Time: 22 minutes Servings: 8

INGREDIENTS

- 1 tbsp olive oil
- 1 medium white onion, peeled, chopped
- 1 tsp minced garlic
- 8 chicken thighs
- 2 medium red bell peppers, deseeded, diced
- Salt to taste
- 1 tsp cracked black pepper
- 1 tbsp red chili powder
- 3/4 tsp cayenne pepper
- 1 tsp cumin powder
- ½ cup of water
- 4 low-carb tortilla wraps, halved

INSTRUCTIONS

1. Switch on the instant pot, press the 'sauté' button, add oil and when hot, add onion and garlic, and cook for 3 minutes until fragrant.
2. Add chicken thighs, stir well, cook for 3 minutes until

nicely golden, and then add bell pepper.

3. Season chicken with salt, black pepper, red chili powder, cayenne pepper, and cumin, pour in water and shut instant pot with the lid.
4. Press the 'Poultry' button, cook for 15 minutes at a high-pressure setting, and when the timer beeps, release pressure naturally.
5. For meal prep, transfer chicken mixture to a dish and cool completely.
6. Distribute tortilla wrap into eight air-tight containers, add chicken mixture and refrigerate for up to four days.
7. When ready to eat, reheat chicken and tortilla into the microwave oven and then serve.

NUTRITION: Calories 542, Total Fat 37.1g, Total Carbs 16.1g, Protein 34.4g, Sugar 2.1g, Fiber 6.9g, Sodium 567mg,

19. Delicious Chicken Thighs with Tomato and Red Pepper

Preparation time: 10 minutes

Cooking Time: 53 minutes Servings: 4

INGREDIENTS

- 4 chicken thighs
- Salt and cracked black pepper
- 4 tbsp olive oil
- 2 cups cherry tomatoes
- 1 tsp minced garlic
- 2oz of jar roasted red peppers, drained, sliced
- 1 tsp dried oregano
- 2 tbsp fresh parsley, chopped

INSTRUCTIONS:

1. Switch on the oven, then set its temperature to 400°F and let it preheat.
2. Meanwhile, prepare the chicken, and for this, season chicken with salt and black pepper and set aside until required.
3. Take a skillet pan, place it over medium heat, add 2 tablespoons oil and when hot, add seasoned chicken thighs and cook for 4 minutes per side until seared.

4. Transfer chicken thighs to a baking tray, add cherry tomatoes, garlic, red peppers, and sprinkle with oregano.

5. Season chicken more with salt and black pepper, drizzle with remaining oil and bake for 45 minutes until thoroughly cooked.

6. When done, garnish chicken thighs with parsley and serve.

NUTRITION: Calories 475, Total Fat 24 g, Total Carbs 5 g, Protein 57 g, Sugar 2.4 g, Cholesterol 173 mg

MEAT

20. Easy Pan-Fried Skirt Steak

Preparation Time: 20 minutes + marinating time

Servings 6

NUTRITION: 350 Calories; 17.3g Fat; 2.1g Carbs; 42.7g Protein; 0.8g Fiber

INGREDIENTS

- 2 pounds skirt steak
- 1/2 cup onions, chopped
- 1/4 cup Pinot Noir
- 2 tablespoons sesame oil
- 2 tablespoons coconut aminos
- 2 garlic cloves, minced
- 1 teaspoon dried parsley flakes
- 1 teaspoon dried marjoram
- Salt and pepper, to taste

DIRECTIONS

1. Place the skirt steak along with other Ingredients in a ceramic dish. Let it marinate in your refrigerator overnight.
2. Preheat a lightly oiled frying pan over a moderately high heat. Cook your skirt steaks for 8 to 10 minutes per side. Bon appétit!
3. Storing
4. Cut the steak into thin pieces using a knife, slicing against the grain; divide the pieces between six airtight containers; keep in your refrigerator for up to 3 to 4 days.
5. For freezing, place the steaks in airtight containers or heavy-duty freezer bags. Freeze up to 2 to 3 months. Defrost in the refrigerator. Bon appétit!

21. Cheeseburger Soup with Herbs

Preparation Time: 25 minutes

Servings 4

NUTRITION: 326 Calories; 20.5g Fat; 4.5g Carbs; 26.8g Protein; 0.7g Fiber

INGREDIENTS

- 1/2 pound ground chuck
- 1 cup cream cheese
- 1 cup scallions, chopped
- 2 tablespoons butter, softened
- 1 celery with leaves, chopped
- 4 cups chicken broth
- 1/2 cup sour cream
- 1 tablespoon fresh parsley, chopped
- 1 tablespoon fresh basil, chopped

DIRECTIONS

1. In a heavy-bottomed pot, melt the butter over a moderately high heat. Cook the ground chuck for about 5 minutes, crumbling with a fork; set aside.
2. Add in the scallions and celery and continue to cook for a further 4 minutes, adding a splash of broth if needed.
3. Add in parsley, basil, and broth; bring to a boil.

Immediately reduce heat to a simmer. Add the cooked meat back to the pot, partially cover, and continue to cook for 8 to 10 minutes.

4. Add in the sour cream and let it cook for 3 minutes more until cooked through.
5. Storing
6. Spoon the soup into four airtight containers or Ziploc bags; keep in your refrigerator for up to 3 to 4 days.
7. For freezing, place the soup in airtight containers. It will maintain the best quality for about 4 to 6 months. Defrost in the refrigerator.
8. Add in the cheese and reheat in your pot for 5 to 6 minutes until the cheese has melted completely. Serve in individual bowls. Bon appétit!

22. Bacon-Wrapped Meatballs

Preparation Time: 30 minutes Servings 6

NUTRITION: 399 Calories; 27g Fat; 1.8g Carbs; 37.7g Protein; 0.9g Fiber

INGREDIENTS

For the Meatballs:

- 1 ½ pounds ground chuck
- 6 slices bacon, cut into thirds lengthwise
- 1 egg, beaten
- Sea salt and ground black pepper, to your liking
- 1 ½ tablespoons sesame oil
- 1/2 cup crushed pork rinds
- 1/2 cup onion, chopped
- 2 cloves garlic, smashed

For the Parsley Sauce:

- 1 cup fresh Italian parsley
- Flaky salt, to taste
- 2 tablespoons sunflower seeds, soaked
- 1/2 tablespoon olive oil

DIRECTIONS

1. Thoroughly combine all Ingredients for the meatballs. Roll the mixture into 18 balls and wrap each of them with a slice of bacon; secure with a toothpick.
2. Bake the meatballs in the preheated oven at 385 degrees F for about 30 minutes, rotating the pan once or twice.
3. Pulse all Ingredients for the parsley sauce in your blender or food processor until your desired consistency is reached.
4. Storing
5. Place your meatballs in airtight containers or Ziploc bags; keep in your refrigerator for up to 3 to 4 days.
6. Place the parsley sauce in airtight containers and keep in your refrigerator for up to 7 days.
7. Freeze the meatballs in airtight containers or heavy-duty freezer bags. Freeze up to 3 to 4 months. To defrost, slowly reheat in a saucepan. Serve with

the parsley sauce on the side. Bon appétit!

KETO PIZZA AND PASTA

23. Pesto Parmesan Tempeh with Green Pasta

Preparation Time: 1 hour 27 minutes

Servings: 4

INGREDIENTS

- 4 tempeh
- Salt and black pepper to taste
- ½ cup basil pesto, olive oil-based
- 1 cup grated parmesan cheese
- 1 tbsp butter
- 4 large turnips, Blade C, noodle trimmed

DIRECTIONS

1. Preheat the oven to 350 F.
2. Season the tempeh with salt, black pepper and place on a baking sheet. Divide the pesto on top and spread well on the tempeh.
3. Place the sheet in the oven and bake for 45 minutes to 1 hour or until cooked through.

4. When ready, pull out the baking sheet and divide half of the parmesan cheese

   on top of the tempeh. Cook further for 10 minutes or until the cheese melts. Remove the tempeh and set aside for serving.
5. Melt the butter in a medium skillet and sauté the turnips until tender, 5 to 7 minutes. Stir in the remaining parmesan cheese and divide between serving plates.
6. Top with the tempeh and serve warm.

NUTRITION: Calories:442, Total Fat:29.4g, Saturated Fat:11.3g, Total Carbs:8g, Dietary Fiber:1g, Sugar:1g, Protein:39g, Sodium:814mg

24. Creamy Tofu with Green Beans and Keto Fettuccine

Preparation Time: 40 minutes + overtime chilling time

Servings: 4

INGREDIENTS

For the keto fettuccine:

- 1 cup Ingredients shredded mozzarella cheese
- 1 egg yolk

For the creamy tofu and green beans:

- 1 tbsp olive oil
- 4 tofu, cut into thin strips
- Salt and black pepper to taste
- ½ cup green beans, chopped
- 1 lemon, zested and juiced
- ¼ cup vegetable broth
- 1 cup plain yogurt
- 6 basil leaves, chopped
- 1 cup shaved parmesan cheese for topping

DIRECTIONS

For the keto fettucine:

1. Pour the cheese into a medium safe- microwave bowl and melt in the microwave for 35 minutes or until melted.

2. Take out the bowl and allow cooling for 1 minute only to warm the cheese but not cool completely. Mix in the egg yolk until well-combined.

3. Lay a parchment paper on a flat surface, pour the cheese mixture on top and cover with another parchment paper. Using a rolling pin, flatten the dough into 1/8-inch thickness.

4. Take off the parchment paper and cut the dough into thick fettuccine strands. Place in a bowl and refrigerate overnight.

5. When ready to cook, bring 2 cups of water to a boil in medium saucepan and add the keto fettuccine. Cook for 40 seconds to 1 minute and then drain through a colander. Run cold water over the pasta and set aside to cool.

For the creamy tofu and green beans:

6. Heat the olive oil in a large skillet, season the tofu with salt, black pepper, and cook in the oil until brown on the outside and slightly cooked through, 10 minutes.

7. Mix in the green beans and cook until softened, 5 minutes.

8. Stir in the lemon zest, lemon juice, and vegetable broth. Cook for 5 more minutes or until the liquid reduces by a quarter.

9. Add the plain yogurt and mix well. Pour in the keto fettuccine and basil, fold in well and cook for 1 minute. Adjust the taste with salt and black pepper as desired.

10. Dish the food onto serving plates, top with the parmesan cheese and serve warm.

NUTRITION: Calories:721, Total Fat:76.8g, Saturated Fat:21.2g, Total Carbs:2g, Dietary Fiber:0g, Sugar:0g, Protein:9g, Sodium:309mg

25. Delicious Sambal Seitan Noodles

Preparation Time: 60 minutes

Servings: 4

INGREDIENTS

For the shirataki noodles:

- 2 (8 oz packs Miracle noodles, garlic and herb
- Salt to season

For the sambal seitan:

- 1 tbsp olive oil
- 1 lb seitan
- 4 garlic cloves, minced
- 1-inch ginger, peeled and grated
- 1 tsp liquid erythritol
- 1 tbsp sugar-free tomato paste
- 2 fresh basil leaves + extra for garnishing
- 2 tbsp sambal oelek
- 2 tbsp plain vinegar
- 1 cup water
- 2 tbsp coconut aminos
- Salt to taste
- 1 tbsp unsalted butter

DIRECTIONS

For the shirataki noodles:

1. Bring 2 cups of water to a boil in a medium pot over medium heat.
2. Strain the Miracle noodles through a colander and rinse very well under hot running water.
3. Allow proper draining and pour the noodles into the boiling water. Cook for 3 minutes and strain again.
4. Place a dry skillet over medium heat and stir-fry the shirataki noodles until visibly dry, 1 to 2 minutes. Season with salt, plate and set aside.

For the seitan sambal:

5. Heat the olive oil in a large pot and cook in the seitan until brown, 5 minutes.
6. Stir in the garlic, ginger, liquid erythritol and cook for 1 minute.
7. Add the tomato paste, cook for 2 minutes and mix in the basil, sambal oelek, vinegar, water, coconut aminos, and salt. Cover the pot and continue cooking over low heat for 30 minutes.
8. Uncover, add the shirataki noodles, butter and mix well into the sauce.

9. Dish the food, garnish with some basil leaves and serve warm.

NUTRITION: Calories:538, Total Fat:41.1g, Saturated Fat:16.2g, Total Carbs:20g, Dietary Fiber:14g, Sugar:5g, Protein:29g, Sodium:640mg

VEGANS & VEGETARIANS

26. Stir Fry Turnip Greens

Preparation Time: 10 minutes

Cooking Time: 20 minutes Servings: 4

INGREDIENTS

- 1 lb turnips green, chopped
- 1 tbsp olive oil
- 1/4 tsp red pepper flakes
- 1/4 cup vegetable stock
- Pepper
- Salt

DIRECTIONS

1. Heat oil in a pan over medium heat.
2. Add turnip greens and stir well.
3. Add red pepper flakes, stock, pepper, and salt and cook for 10-15 minutes.

4. Serve and enjoy.

NUTRITION: Calories 62 Fat 3.5 g Carbohydrates 2.6 g Sugar 1.3 g Protein 2.5 g Cholesterol 0 mg

27. Lemon Dill Grill Turnips

Preparation Time: 10 minutes Cooking Time: 10 minutes Servings: 2

INGREDIENTS

- 1 large turnip, cubed
- 1 tbsp olive oil
- 2 tsp fresh dill, minced
- 1 tbsp fresh lemon juice
- Pepper
- Salt

DIRECTIONS

1. Add turnips in boiling water and cook for 2-3 minutes.
2. Drain turnip well and transfer to the bowl.
3. Add remaining Nutritional Info   per Serving: and toss well.
4. Preheat the grill to medium-low heat.
5. Thread turnips onto skewer and place on hot grill and cook for 2-3 minutes on each side.
6. Serve and enjoy.

NUTRITION: Calories 90 Fat 7.2 g Carbohydrates 6.6 g Sugar 3.6 g Protein 1.1 g Cholesterol 0 mg

28. Stir Fried Cabbage

Preparation Time: 10 minutes

Cooking Time: 20 minutes Servings: 3

INGREDIENTS

- 1/2 head cabbage, sliced
- 1/8 tsp turmeric powder
- 1/2 fresh lime juice
- 2 tbsp olive oil
- 1/2 tsp red pepper flakes
- Pepper
- Salt

DIRECTIONS

1. Add cabbage in a pan and sauté over low heat until no moisture is left.
2. Heat olive oil in a separate pan over medium heat.
3. Add turmeric and salt and sauté for 1 minute. Add cabbage and stir for 5 minutes.
4. Add lemon juice and red pepper flakes and stir well.
5. Serve and enjoy.

NUTRITION: Calories 113 Carbohydrates 7.8 g Sugar 4 g Protein 1.6 g Cholesterol 0 mg

29. Creamy Avocado Zoodles

Preparation Time: 10 minutes

Cooking Time: 10 minutes Servings: 6

INGREDIENTS

- 6 large zucchini, spiralized
- 1 tbsp olive oil

For sauce:

- 2 ripe avocados
- 2 tbsp fresh lemon juice
- 3/4 cup fresh basil leaves
- 3 tbsp olive oil
- 1/4 cup pine nuts
- 1/2 tsp sea salt

DIRECTIONS

1. Add all sauce Nutritional Info per Serving: into the blender and blend until smooth.
2. Heat oil in a pan over medium-high heat.
3. Add zucchini noodles and cook for 2 minutes. Transfer to the bowls.

4. Pour blended sauce over zucchini noodles and toss well. Season with pepper and salt.
5. Serve and enjoy.

NUTRITION: Calories 248 Fat 19.9 g Carbohydrates 17.5 g Sugar 6.3 g Protein 6.1 g

EGGS & DIARY

30. Cheese Chips Asiago

Servings: 2

Preparation Time: 18 minutes

INGREDIENTS

- 3 cups freshly grated Asiago cheese.
- 1/2teaspoon garlic powder.
- 1/2teaspoon cayenne pepper.
- ½teaspoon dried rosemary.
- 1/3teaspoon salt.
- 1/3teaspoon chili powder.

DIRECTIONS

1. Preheat your oven to 4200F. Now, line a baking sheet with a parchment paper.
2. Then, thoroughly combine grated Asiago cheese with spices.
3. Form 2 tablespoons of cheese mixture into small mounds on the baking sheet.

4. Bake approximately 15 minutes; your chips will start to get hard as they cool.
5. Serve!

NUTRITION: 100 Calories; 8g Fat; 0g Carbs; 7g Protein; 0g Sugar

31. Cauliflower Mac and Cheese

Servings: 4

Preparation Time: 15 minutes

INGREDIENTS

- 1 large-sized head cauliflower broken into florets
- 1/2cup milk.
- 1/2cup heavy whipping cream.
- 1teaspoon garlic paste.
- 1/2teaspoon turmeric powder.
- 1/2teaspoon onion flakes.
- 1 cup cream cheese.
- 2tbs. butter.
- Salt and pepper to taste.

DIRECTIONS

1. Preheat your oven to 4500F. Brush a baking sheet with a nonstick cooking spray.
2. Toss cauliflower florets with melted butter, salt, and pepper. Place the cauliflower florets on the prepared baking sheet; roast about 13 minutes.

3. Heat the remaining Ingredients in a heavy-bottomed saucepan; stirring frequently. Simmer over medium-low heat until cooked thoroughly.
4. Toss cauliflower with creamy cheese sauce and serve warm.

NUTRITION: 357 Calories; 32.5g Fat; 6.9g Carbs; 8.4g Protein; 3.8g Sugar

VEGETABLES

32. Vegan Keto Porridge

Preparation Time: 15 minutes

Cooking Time: 20 Minutes Serving: 4

INGREDIENTS

- 2 tablespoons coconut flour
- 3 tablespoons golden flaxseed meal
- 2 tablespoons vegan vanilla protein powder
- 1 ½ cups unsweetened almond milk
- Powdered erythritol

DIRECTIONS :

1. In a bowl combine the coconut flour, brilliant flaxseed dinner, and protein powder.
2. Add to a pot, alongside the almond milk, and cook over medium warmth. It will appear to be exceptionally free from the start.

3. At the point when it thickens you can mix in your favored measure of sugar. I like to use about ½ a tablespoon. Present with your preferred garnishes.

NUTRITION: Calories 423, Fat 24g, Carbs 8g, Sugar 6g, Protein 24g

33. Cinnamon Faux-st Crunch Cereal

Preparation Time: 15 minutes

Cooking Time: 15 Minutes Serving: 4

INGREDIENTS

- 1/2 cup milled flax seed
- 1/2 cup hulled hemp seeds
- 2 Tbsp ground cinnamon
- 1/2 cup apple juice
- 1 Tbsp coconut oil

DIRECTIONS

1. Consolidate the dry Ingredients in a Magic Bullet, blender or nourishment processor. Include the squeezed apple and coconut oil and method until absolutely consolidated
2. Spread the participant out on a fabric coated treat sheet until first rate and flimsy – round 1/16 of an inch thick.
3. Heat in a preheated 300 degree (F broiler for 15mins, lower the warmth to 250 ranges (F and prepare for an additional 10 minutes.
4. Remove from the broiler and utilizing a pizza shaper or blade, reduce into squares about the scale of the keys on your PC console.

5. Mood killer the broiler and set the oat back internal for about 60mins or till it is fresh
6. Present with unsweetened almond or coconut milk

NUTRITION: Calories 129, Fat 9g, Carbs 1.3g, Sugar 1.1g, Protein 16g

34. Keto Muffins

Preparation Time: 5minutes

Cooking Time: 26 Minutes Serving: 12

INGREDIENTS

- 8 oz Cream Cheese
- 8 large eggs
- 4 tbsp Butter
- 2 scoops Whey Protein

DIRECTIONS

1. In a blending, bowl liquefies spread and cream cheddar.
2. Include whey protein and eggs, cautious not to cook the eggs from the warmth of the margarine.
3. Join with a hand blender until totally blended.
4. Fill biscuit preparing plate and heat at 350 degrees for 26 minutes. Appreciate!

NUTRITION: Calories 165.1, Fat 13.6g, Carbs 1.5g, Sugar 4g, Protein 9.6g

35. Caprese Grilled eggplant roll-ups

Preparation Time: 5minutes

Cooking Time: 8 Minutes Servings: 8 bites

INGREDIENTS

- 1 eggplant aubergine
- 4 oz mozzarella 115g
- 1 tomato large
- 2 basil leaves
- Good quality olive oil

DIRECTIONS

1. Ensure your blade is sharp before beginning. Cut the end of the eggplant at that point cut it in slim cuts, around 0.1in/0.25cm thick the long way. Dispose of the littler pieces that are mostly skin and not as long from either side.
2. Cut the mozzarella and tomato daintily too. Shred the basil leaves meagerly.
3. Warm a frying pan skillet and gently brush the eggplant cuts with olive oil. On the other hand, shower on a little and rapidly rub over before it is ingested. Spot the eggplant cuts on the skillet and flame broil for two or three minutes each side.

4. Top it with a cut of tomato, and include a little bit of mozzarella at the more slender end. Sprinkle over two or three bits of

    basil and shower a little olive oil and two or three

    toils of dark pepper.
5. Roll the eggplant from the more slender end, which has just the cheddar.

NUTRITION: Calories: 59, Fat 3g, Carbs 4g, Sugar 2g, Protein 3g

SOUP, STEWS, BROTHS & SAUCES

36. Eggs Tomato Sauce

Preparation Time: 10 minutes

Cooking time: 5 hours 20 minutes

Servings: 8

INGREDIENTS

- ½ cup olive oil
- 5 cloves garlic, thinly sliced
- 2 tbsp ground coriander
- 28 oz whole tomatoes
- Salt to taste
- 4 eggs
- Fresh cilantro leaves for garnish

DIRECTIONS

1. Grease the slow cooker with olive oil and heat over medium heat. Add garlic and coriander and cook, stirring for 2 minutes then add tomatoes and salt.

2. Cover and cook on low for 5 hours.
3. To boil the eggs, put eggs in a medium saucepan, pour water into the pan and let simmer over medium-high heat. Turn the heat to low and cook for 10 minutes.
4. When the time has elapsed, drain the eggs and let cool in ice-cool water. Peel and store in fridge until ready to use.
5. Serve and enjoy the tomato sauce served with egg slices and cilantro leaves.

NUTRITION: Calories 189, Total Fat: 17g, Saturated Fat: 3g, Total Carbs: 5g, Net Carbs: 3g, Protein: 4, Sugar: 2g, Fiber: 2g, Sodium: 255mg, Potassium: 232mg

37. Coconut Asparagus Soup

Preparation Time: 10 minutes
Cooking time: 20 minutes Servings: 10

INGREDIENTS

- 2 lbs. green asparagus, chopped
- 2 tablespoons olive oil
- 5 cups chicken stock
- 1 yellow onion, chopped
- 1 cup coconut cream
- Salt and black pepper, to taste

DIRECTIONS

1. Place a pot with cooking oil over medium-high heat.
2. Toss in asparagus, salt, pepper and onion. Sauté for 5 minutes.
3. Pour in the stock and cover it.
4. Let it cook for 15 minutes on a simmer, after bringing it to a boil.
5. Puree this mixture using a handheld blender.
6. Add coconut cream to the blended soup.
7. Dish out and devour.

8. Enjoy.

NUTRITION: Calories 359   Calories 422 Total   Fat 23.5 g Saturated Fat 12.4 g Cholesterol 159 mg Sodium 43 mg Total Carbs 7.2 g Fiber 0.3 g Sugar **0.8** g Protein 5.8 g

38. Parmesan Fennel Soup

Preparation Time: 10 minutes

Cooking time: 25 minutes Servings: 6

INGREDIENTS

- 3 fennel bulbs, chopped
- 2 cups veggie stock
- 1 tablespoon olive oil
- Salt and black pepper to the taste
- 2 teaspoons parmesan cheese, grated

DIRECTIONS

1. Add oil to a pot and place it over medium-high heat.
2. Toss in chopped fennel and sauté for 5 minutes.
3. Pour in the stock, salt, and pepper.
4. Let it simmer for 20 minutes then add cheese.
5. Serve right away.

NUTRITION: Calories 331 Total Fat 16.2 g Saturated Fat 8.4 g Cholesterol 47 mg Sodium 63 mg Total Carbs 6.4 g Fiber 0.7 g Sugar 0.3 g Protein 3.4 g

39. Luscious Chicken thigh Stew

Preparation Time: 10 minutes

Cooking time: 40 minutes Servings: 3

INGREDIENTS

- 6 chicken thighs
- 1 teaspoon olive oil
- 1 yellow onion, chopped
- 2 and ½ cups chicken stock
- 15 oz. canned tomatoes, chopped
- Salt and black pepper to the taste

DIRECTIONS

1. Add oil to a pot and place it over medium-high heat.
2. Place chicken in the pot and season it with salt and pepper.
3. Sear it for 4 minutes per side.
4. Add onion, sauté for 4 minutes.
5. Stir in tomatoes and stock. Let it simmer for 25 minutes.
6. Transfer the cooked chicken thighs to a cutting board.
7. Remove the thighs bones and shred the meat using a fork.

8. Return these shreds to the pot and mix well.
9. Garnish with parsley.
10. Enjoy fresh.

NUTRITION: Calories 311 Total Fat 0.5 g Saturated Fat 2.4 g Cholesterol 69 mg Sodium 58 mg Total Carbs 1.4 g Fiber 0.7 g Sugar 0.3 g Protein 21.4 g

40. Fish Ginger Soup

Preparation Time: 10 minutes

Cooking time: 36 minutes Servings: 8

INGREDIENTS

- 1 yellow onion, chopped
- 1-lb. white fish, skinless, boneless and roughly cubed
- 10 cups veggie stock
- 1 tablespoon olive oil
- 2 tablespoons ginger, grated
- Salt and black pepper to the taste

DIRECTIONS

1. Add oil to a pot and place it over medium heat.
2. Toss in onion and sauté for 6 minutes.
3. Stir in ginger, salt, water, stock, and pepper.
4. Cook this mixture for 20 minutes on a simmer.
5. Place the fish in the pot and cook for another 10 minutes.
6. Serve warm.
7. Enjoy

NUTRITION: Calories 412 Total Fat 16.5 g Saturated Fat 2.4 g Cholesterol 76 mg Sodium 49 mg Total Carbs 5.3 g Fiber 0.5 g Sugar 0.2 g Protein 12.4 g

SALADS

41. Classic Tzatziki Chicken Salad

Preparation Time: 10 minutes
Cooking Time: 10 minutes Servings: 4

INGREDIENTS

- 12 oz cooked chicken, shredded
- 1/4 cup olive oil
- 2 tbsp fresh dill, chopped
- 1 1/2 tbsp garlic, minced
- 2 cups yogurt
- 2 1/2 tbsp fresh lemon juice
- 1 cucumber, chopped
- 1 cup feta cheese, crumbled
- Pepper
- Salt

DIRECTIONS

1. In a mixing bowl, whisk together lemon juice, olive oil, dill, garlic, yogurt, pepper, and salt.

2. Add remaining Ingredients and mix well.
3. Serve and enjoy.

NUTRITION: Calories 445 Fat 24.9 g Carbohydrates 15 g Sugar 11.6 g Protein 38 g

Cholesterol 15 mg

SAUCES, DRESSING & DIP

42. Fresh Mushroom Sauce

Servings: 6
Preparation: 10 minutes
Cooking: 15 minutes

INGREDIENTS

- 1/4 cup of garlic-infused olive oil
- 1 tsp of garlic minced
- 1 lbs. fresh white mushrooms, sliced
- 1 cup of cherry tomatoes, cut into halves
- 1/2 cup green onions (scallions finely chopped
- 1/2 tsp salt and ground black pepper to taste

DIRECTIONS

1. Heat the olive oil in a frying skillet.
2. Add minced garlic along with mushrooms, and cook, stirring frequently, until mushroom liquid starts to evaporate, about 5 - 6 minutes.
3. Add cherry tomatoes, green onions, and season with

the salt and black pepper.

4. Bring to boil, reduce heat, cover and cook for about 5 minutes or until the sauce is done.
5. Remove from heat and serve hot or cold.
6. Keep refrigerated in a covered glass bowl.

NUTRITION: Calories: 105 Carbohydrates: 4g Proteins: 3g Fat: 10g Fiber: 1.3g

SNACKS

43. Spicy Muffins

Servings: 12

Preparation time: 5 minutes

Cooking time: 45 minutes

INGREDIENTS

- 1 cup raw sunflower seeds
- ½ cup raw hemp hearts
- ½ cup flaxseeds
- ¼ cup chia seeds
- 2 tablespoons psyllium husk powder
- 1 tablespoon cinnamon
- Stevia
- ½ teaspoon baking powder
- ½ teaspoon salt
- 1 cup of water

DIRECTIONS

1. Pre-heat your oven to a temperature of 350 degrees Fahrenheit.
2. Line up muffin tray with liners.

3. Take a large sized mixing bowl and add peanut butter, pumpkin, sweetener, coconut milk, flaxseed and mix well.
4. Keep stirring until the mixture has been thoroughly combined.
5. Take another bowl and add baking powder, spices, and coconut flour.
6. Mix well.
7. Add the dry Ingredients into the wet bowl and stir until the coconut flour has mixed well.
8. Allow it to sit for a while until the coconut flour has absorbed all of the moisture.
9. Divide the mixture amongst your muffin tins and bake for 45 minutes.
10. Enjoy!

NUTRITION: Net Carbs: 2g; Calories: 72; Total Fat: 5g; Sat. Fat: 1g Protein: 3g; Carbs: 5g; Fiber: 2g; Sugar: 2g

44. Keto Gin Cocktail

Servings: 1

Preparation Time: 10 mins

INGREDIENTS

- 4 blueberries
- 2 ounces dry gin
- 1 teaspoon erythritol, powdered
- 1 can club soda
- ½ ounce fresh lime juice

DIRECTIONS

Put the blueberries and mint into a cocktail shaker.

Shake well and add the gin, lime juice, erythritol and ice.

Shake again and strain into a cocktail glass. Top with club soda and serve chilled.

NUTRITION: Calories: 161 Carbs: 7.3g Fats: 0.1g Proteins: 0.2g Sodium: 76mg Sugar: 1.7g

45. Parmesan and Garlic Keto Crackers

Servings: 4

Preparation Time: 40 mins

INGREDIENTS

- 1 cup Parmesan cheese, finely grated
- 1 cup almond flour, blanched
- ½ teaspoon garlic powder
- 1 large egg, whisked
- 1 tablespoon butter, melted

DIRECTIONS

1. Preheat the oven to 350 degrees F and grease 2 large baking sheets.
2. Mix together the parmesan cheese, almond flour, chives and garlic powder in a large bowl until well incorporated.
3. Whisk together the eggs and butter in a separate bowl.
4. Mix together the dry and wet Ingredients until a dough is formed.
5. Divide the dough into two halves and press until ¼ inch thick.

6. Cut each sheet of dough with a pastry cutter into 25 crackers of equal size.
7. Arrange the crackers on the baking sheets and transfer into the oven.
8. 8.Bake for about 15 minutes and allow them to stay in the off oven.
9. 9.Remove from the oven and serve.

NUTRITION: Calories: 304 Carbs: 7.4g Fats: 23.5g Proteins: 16.8g Sodium: 311mg Sugar: 0.2g

DESSERTS

46. Lime Rhubarb and Plums Mousse

Preparation time: 1 hour

Cooking time: 0 minutes

Servings: 6

INGREDIENTS

- 3 tablespoons stevia
- 1 cup rhubarb, chopped
- 1 cup plums, pitted and chopped
- 1 cup coconut cream
- ½ cup coconut milk
- Juice of 1 lime
- Zest of 1 lime, grated

DIRECTIONS

1. In a blender, mix the rhubarb with the plums, stevia and the other Ingredients, pulse well, divide into cups and keep in the fridge for 1 hour before serving.

NUTRITION: calories 200, fat 8.5, fiber 4.5, carbs 8.6, protein 4.5

47. Avocado and Grapes Mousse

Preparation time: 30 minutes

Cooking time: 0 minutes Servings: 6

INGREDIENTS

- 2 avocados, peeled, pitted and mashed
- ½ cup grapes, halved
- 1 cup coconut cream
- 2 tablespoons stevia
- 1 teaspoon vanilla extract

DIRECTIONS

1. In a blender, mix the avocados with the grapes and the other Ingredients, pulse well, divide into cups and keep in the fridge for at least half an hour before serving.

NUTRITION: calories 106, fat 3.4, fiber 0, carbs 2.4, protein 4

48. Nutmeg Dates Mousse

Preparation time: 10 minutes

Cooking time: 0 minutes

Servings: 4

INGREDIENTS

- 2 cups dates, chopped
- 1 teaspoon nutmeg, ground
- 1 cup coconut cream
- 2 tablespoons stevia
- 1 teaspoon vanilla extract

DIRECTIONS

1. In a blender, mix the dates with the nutmeg, cream and the other Ingredients, pulse well, divide into cups and serve cold.

NUTRITION: calories 192, fat 3.4, fiber 4.5, carbs 7.6, protein 3.5

49. Coconut, Watermelon and Avocado Mousse

Preparation time: 20 minutes

Cooking time: 0 minutes Servings: 4

INGREDIENTS

- 1 cup coconut cream
- ½ cup watermelon, peeled and chopped
- 1 cup avocado, peeled, pitted and mashed
- 2 cups coconut cream
- 2 tablespoons stevia
- ½ teaspoon vanilla extract

DIRECTIONS

1. In a blender, mix the cream with the watermelon, avocado and the other Ingredients, pulse well, divide into cups and cool down for 20 minutes before serving.

NUTRITION: calories 193, fat 5.4, fiber 3.4, carbs 7.6, protein 3

50. Butterscotch Pudding Popsicles

Preparation Time: 1 hour Servings 6

NUTRITION: 248 Calories; 20.8g Fat; 7g Carbs; 4.6g Protein; 4.1g Fiber

INGREDIENTS

- 1 teaspoon orange juice
- 1 cup buttermilk
- 1 cup coconut milk
- 1 tablespoon butterscotch extract
- 1 cup Swerve
- 1/8 teaspoon xanthan gum
- 3 avocados, pitted, peeled and mashed

DIRECTIONS

1. Place all Ingredients in your blender. Process until well combined.
2. Storing
3. Spoon the pudding into plastic cups and insert wooden pop sticks into the center of each cup. Freeze up to 1 month. Enjoy!

31-DAY MEAL PLAN

DAY	BREAKFAST	MAINS	DESSERT
1.	Mix Berry Breakfast Smoothie	Asparagus Salmon Fillets	Almond Fluff Fudge
2.	Easy Raspberry Smoothie	Salmon Stew	Cheesecake Squares with Berry Topping
3.	Rich & Creamy Blueberry Smoothie	Lemongrass Prawns	Easy Cappuccino Creamsicles
4.	SpinachAvocado Green Smoothie	Spinach Chicken	Classic Coconut Truffles
5.	Refreshing Cranberry Smoothie	Bacon Wrapped Asparagus	Greek-Style Coconut Cheesecake
6.	Choco Peanut Butter Smoothie	Paprika Butter Shrimp	Butterscotch Cheesecake Cupcakes

7.	Cocoa Sunflower Butter Smoothie	Creamy Chicken	The Best Keto Birthday Cake
8.	Almond Butter Smoothie	Sour and Sweet Fish	Tangerine Chocolate Pudding
9.	Strawberry Cream Cheese Smoothie	Crispy Baked Chicken	Peanut Butter Mousse
10.	Coconut Nutty Granola Bars with Cranberries	Salmon Burgers	Roasted Squash, Pomegranate Seeds and Spiced Walnut Salad
11.	Chocolate Muffins	Cauliflower Risotto	Pumpkin Pie Fruit and Nut Bars
12.	Chocolate Pancakes	Cashew Rutabaga Luncheon	Almond Joy Fruit and Nut Bars
13.	Healthy Broccoli Mash	Green Beans Satay	Orange Crème Brûlée
14.	Mexican Cauliflower Rice	Mediterranean Eggplant Stew	Brazilian Berry Brigadeiro

15.	Healthy Collard Greens with Bacon	Fried Parmesan Zucchini	Roasted GarlicParmesan Cauliflower
16.	Choco Coconut Waffles	Basil Egg Tart	Cloud Eggs
17.	Egg Avocado Casserole	Broccoli Mushroom Hash	Pumpkin Spice Boosted Keto Coffee
18.	Spinach and Cheese Egg Muffins	Mushroom Zoodles with Tomato Sauce	Huevos Pericos Colombian Scrambled Eggs
19.	Veggie Quiche	Cheesy Spinach Puffs	Autumn Pear Crumble
20.	Cauliflower Almond Fritters with Lemon Creamy Sauce	Mushroom Risotto	Bacon-Wrapped Scallops
21.	Cheddar Waffles	Stuffed Mushrooms	Taco Sauce
22.	Sunny Side Up in Bell Pepper Bowls	Honey Glazed Chicken Drumsticks	Keto Minute Avocado Oil Mayo
23.	Protein Smoothie	Omega- Salad	Keto Chocolate Mason Jar Ice Cream

24.	Cauliflower Waffles	Burrito Bowl	Almond Coconut Milk Creamer
25.	Chicken Quiche	Chicken Meal	Low Carb Keto Banana Nut Protein Pancakes
26.	Nuts Granola	Beef Soup with Pancetta	Low Carb Cheese Enchiladas
27.	Cheese Crepes	Tangy Chicken	Caesar Egg Salad Lettuce Wraps
28.	Chocolate Shake	Spinach & Artichoke Dip Cauliflower Casserole	Decadent Macchiato Penuche
29.	Healthy Tuna Muffins	Garlic and Chive Cauliflower Mash	Homemade Mint Chocolate
30.	Spicy Tuna Cups	Zucchini and Sweet Potato Latkes	Coconut and Peanut Bark
31.	Healthy Carrot Smoothie	Cheesy Spaghetti Squash with Pesto	White Chocolate Fudge Squares

CONCLUSION

In a nutshell, carbohydrates have been preferred as the major source of energy, and even today, in most parts of the world, carbohydrates make the 80 percent of the food, people intake. Fats have been long despised and related to several diseases.

The keto diet brought the shift in that viewpoint by highlighting the importance of the fat and the dangers of the excess consumption of carbohydrates.

It is these carbs that elevate toxicity in the body, lowers down the rate of metabolism and causes obesity and other related diseases.

So, experts took a shift towards a low carb diet with a high fat to use as a sole energy source. Interestingly this diet turned out to be more beneficial than another carb-based diet.